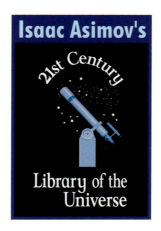

Isaac Asimov's
21st Century
Library of the Universe

The Solar System

The Sun

BY ISAAC ASIMOV

WITH REVISIONS AND UPDATING BY RICHARD HANTULA

Gareth Stevens Publishing
A WORLD ALMANAC EDUCATION GROUP COMPANY

Please visit our web site at: **www.garethstevens.com**
For a free color catalog describing Gareth Stevens Publishing's list of high-quality
books and multimedia programs, call 1-800-542-2595 (USA) or 1-800-387-3178 (Canada).
Gareth Stevens Publishing's fax: (414) 332-3567.

Library of Congress Cataloging-in-Publication Data

Asimov, Isaac.
    The sun / by Isaac Asimov; with revisions and updating by Richard Hantula.
      p. cm. — (Isaac Asimov's 21st century library of the universe. The solar system)
    Rev. ed. of: Sun and its secrets. 1994.
    Summary: A description of the sun, the star of our solar system, which includes information
on its origin, physical composition, and characteristics, as well as on studies made of the sun by
instruments and satellites.
    Includes bibliographical references and index.
    ISBN 0-8368-3242-6 (lib. bdg.)
    1. Sun—Juvenile literature. [1. Sun.] I. Hantula, Richard. II. Asimov, Isaac. Sun and its
secrets. III. Title. IV. Isaac Asimov's 21st century library of the universe. Solar system.
QB521.5.A84 2002
523.7—dc21   2002066807

This edition first published in 2002 by
Gareth Stevens Publishing
A World Almanac Education Group Company
330 West Olive Street, Suite 100
Milwaukee, WI 53212 USA

Series editor: Betsy Rasmussen
Cover design and layout adaptation: Melissa Valuch
Picture research: Kathy Keller
Additional picture research: Diane Laska-Swanke
Artwork commissioning: Kathy Keller and Laurie Shock
Production director: Susan Ashley

The editors at Gareth Stevens Publishing have selected science author Richard Hantula to bring
this classic series of young people's information books up to date. Richard Hantula has written
and edited books and articles on science and technology for more than two decades. He was
the senior U.S. editor for the *Macmillan Encyclopedia of Science*.

In addition to Hantula's contribution to this most recent edition, the editors would like to
acknowledge the participation of two noted science authors, Greg Walz-Chojnacki and
Francis Reddy, as contributors to earlier editions of this work.

Printed in the United States of America

1 2 3 4 5 6 7 8 9 06 05 04 03 02

Contents

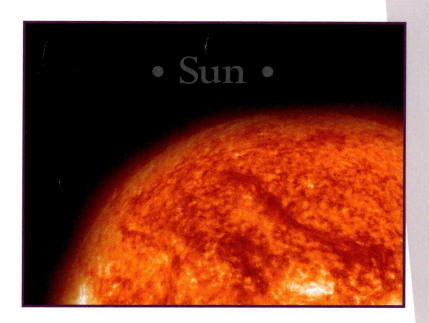

• Sun •

We live in an enormously large place – the Universe. It is only natural that we would want to understand this place, so scientists and engineers have developed instruments and spacecrafts that have told us far more about the Universe than we could possibly imagine.

We have seen planets up close, and spacecrafts have even landed on some. We have learned about quasars and pulsars, super-novas and colliding galaxies, and black holes and dark matter. We have gathered amazing data about how the Universe may have come into being and how it may end. Nothing could be more astonishing.

Of all the portions of the Universe we see in the sky, the most spectacular is the Sun. When it is shining, it drowns out everything else. It is so bright, we cannot look at it directly. In fact, we had better not try, because it can quickly damage our eyes. When the Sun shines, all is bright. When clouds cover the Sun, the day is gloomy. At night, when the Sun is not overhead, the sky is dark. All the world depends on the Sun.

Origins of the Sun and Planets

Scientists think the Sun and planets originated about 5 billion years ago in the heart of a cloud of gas and dust. A portion of the cloud began to contract or compress. This loose ball of gas and dust kept contracting as gravity pulled material toward its center, and its temperature gradually increased. Meanwhile, leftover gas and dust gathered in a disk-shaped cloud that rotated around the ball. Eventually, the temperature deep inside the gas ball reached millions of degrees, and the ball began generating its own energy. Our Sun had begun to shine. Within the disk surrounding the newborn Sun, smaller clumps of material took shape. These clumps would become the planets, moons, comets, and asteroids of our Solar System.

Birth of the Sun in a cloud of gas and dust

1. Billions of years ago, part of the cloud began to contract into a ball of gas.

2. Continuing contraction heated the glowing ball of gas.

3. Deep inside the gas ball, temperatures rose so high that nuclear reactions began to produce energy. The Sun was born.

4. Planets, moons, comets, and asteroids formed as the Sun was created. They continue to orbit the Sun today.

The Great Nebula in the constellation Orion glows with the light of hot, young stars. Behind the colorful nebula lies a dark, dusty cloud in which new stars are born. Scientists think our Sun formed in such a cloud.

The explosion of a hydrogen bomb. Like this bomb, the Sun uses hydrogen to produce enormous energy.

Left: A neutrino detector allows scientists to trap and count tiny particles from the Sun called neutrinos.

Above: A NASA image showing a map of the circulation under a sunspot. The picture was made in 2001 with the help of the Michelson Doppler Imager aboard the *Solar and Heliospheric Observatory* (*SOHO*) spacecraft.

What Makes the Sun Shine?

We know that the Sun has existed for billions of years, but what makes it shine? The Sun's energy comes from nuclear reactions that occur deep inside it. The Sun is about three-quarters hydrogen. Its center is so hot and dense that hydrogen atoms can fuse to form another chemical element — helium. Each second, the Sun transforms about 700 million tons of hydrogen into 695 million tons of helium. What becomes of the missing material? It is changed into the energy that heats and lights our star. One day scientists hope to control these same reactions to produce energy from the hydrogen in water here on Earth.

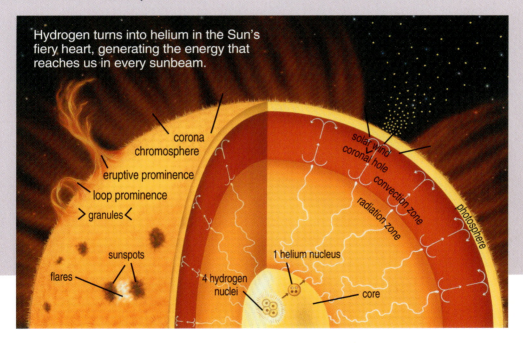

Hydrogen turns into helium in the Sun's fiery heart, generating the energy that reaches us in every sunbeam.

corona
chromosphere
eruptive prominence
loop prominence
> granules <
sunspots
flares
4 hydrogen nuclei
1 helium nucleus
core
solar wind
coronal hole
convection zone
radiation zone
photosphere

The case of the missing neutrinos

When hydrogen fuses to form helium inside the Sun, tiny particles called neutrinos are produced. These fly out of the Sun in all directions. They are very hard to detect, but in the 1960s, scientists developed a way to trap these neutrinos. The number trapped, however, was only $1/3$ the number expected. The experiment was repeated over and over, and each time there was a neutrino shortage. Scientists started to wonder whether they had the wrong idea about what goes on inside the Sun. Finally, in 2001, an experiment suggested that something happened to the neutrinos on their way to Earth. Some of them apparently changed into types of neutrinos that were not detected in the original experiments.

Our Massive and Powerful Sun

The brilliant star that we call our Sun is huge. It is, on average, about 93 million miles (150 million kilometers) away from Earth. At that distance, it *must* be huge to be seen as such a large ball. It is about 865,000 miles (1,392,000 km) in diameter, 109 times as wide as Earth. It has 332,950 times the mass of Earth. In fact, it has almost 1,000 times the combined mass of all the planets, satellites, asteroids, and comets circling it. The Sun's gravitational pull is so strong that it holds all those objects in orbit and forces them to move around it. Our Earth is one of those planets traveling around the Sun. It makes one complete circle in a year.

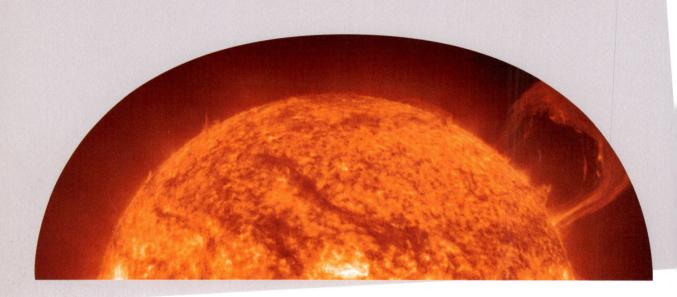

Our Earth-Moon system — tiny beside the Sun!

Here is one way to think about the Sun's size. Imagine that Earth is placed in the center of the Sun. Also imagine that the Moon is circling Earth at its average distance of 238,900 miles (384,400 km) away. As the Moon circles, it would still be inside the Sun. In fact, it would be only a little over halfway to the Sun's surface. In other words, the Sun alone is bigger than the entire Earth-Moon system. Astronauts have traveled from Earth to the Moon, but they have not yet gone far enough to match the distance from the Sun's center to the Sun's surface.

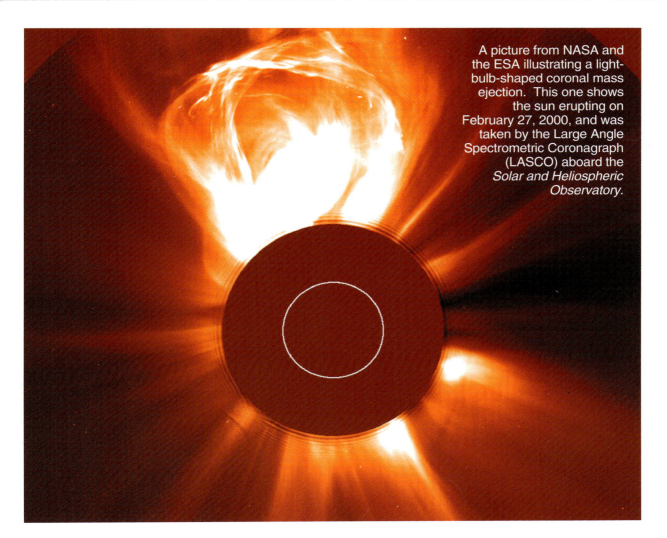

A picture from NASA and the ESA illustrating a light-bulb-shaped coronal mass ejection. This one shows the sun erupting on February 27, 2000, and was taken by the Large Angle Spectrometric Coronagraph (LASCO) aboard the *Solar and Heliospheric Observatory.*

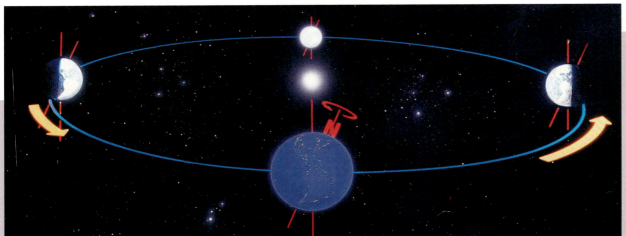

Above: As Earth revolves around, or orbits, the Sun, the northern and southern ends of Earth's axis take turns tilting toward the Sun. Summer comes to the hemisphere that tilts toward the Sun; winter comes to the hemisphere that tilts away from the Sun.

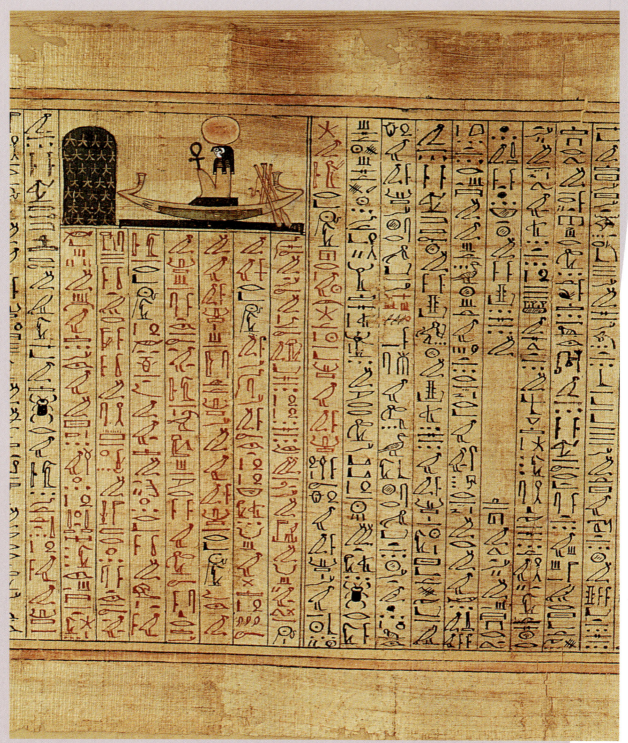

Above: Ra, the Sun god of ancient Egyptian mythology, was usually shown with a hawk's head on a human body. Mythology says that he controlled the Universe by rowing the Sun across the sky in his boat, taking the world from day to night and back to day again.

Sun Worship

Why do we need this powerful star? At night in ancient times, our world was dark except for the dim light of a campfire or the Moon. It was also cold, especially in the winter and especially when the campfire burned low. How relieved people were when the Sun finally rose. The light came, and Earth was heated again.

When you think about the Sun's light and warmth, it is no wonder many ancient people worshiped it as a god. They had good reason. Without the Sun, everything would freeze, and plants that provide food would not grow. Without the Sun, in fact, there would be no life on Earth.

Many ancient religions thought that the creation of the world was made possible by the power of the Sun and its gods.

Our Sun: not too big, not too small — just right!

The more massive a star, the shorter its lifetime. A massive star has more of the hydrogen that stars use in the fusion process to create energy. The hydrogen in a massive star must fuse very rapidly to produce the energy to keep the star from collapsing under its own gravitational pull. An extremely massive star might survive only 100 million years. Then it would explode and collapse. That is not enough time for life to develop. A very small star, on the other hand, might last 200 billion years, but a small star would not produce enough energy for life to develop. Our middle-sized star, the Sun, is just right. It not only produces enough energy for life, but scientists expect it will survive for a total of 10 billion years.

In Constant Motion

The Sun's surface is not even. Parts of it are always rising, and other parts are sinking. It is a little bit like the water of Earth's oceans that rises and falls in waves. As a result of this rising and falling, the surface of the Sun seems to consist of granules of matter packed closely together. A granule of the Sun looks small to us from Earth, but on the average, each one is about 600 miles (1,000 km) across. Although large, a granule does not live long. Each lasts about 8 minutes. Then a new one forms, just as bubbles keep replacing one another in a pan of boiling water. Scientists think there are about 4 million granules on the Sun's surface at any one time.

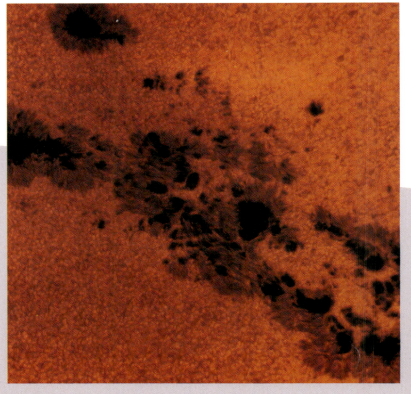

Right: The Sun's granules may look small, but each of the "tiny" grains averages about 600 miles (1,000 km) in diameter.

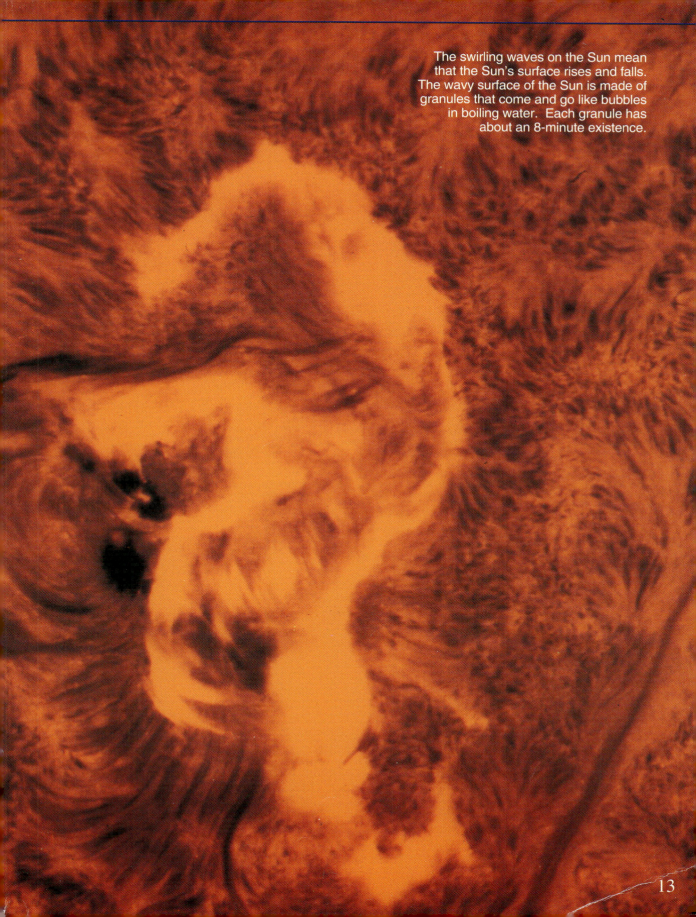

The swirling waves on the Sun mean that the Sun's surface rises and falls. The wavy surface of the Sun is made of granules that come and go like bubbles in boiling water. Each granule has about an 8-minute existence.

13

A Ball of Fire

The temperature at the Sun's surface is about 11,000° Fahrenheit (6,000° Centigrade). At the center, the temperature is about 27,000,000° F (15,000,000° C). This central heat leaks outward very slowly. On the Sun's surface, the heat energy is very active. Here and there, the hot gases expand and become cooler. Cooler gases shine less brightly than hot gases, so some areas appear dark. A dark region is a sunspot. The number of sunspots on the Sun varies. Some years there may be a few hundred sunspots and other years fewer than ten.

In areas around sunspots, the gases are more active. Explosions near these spots give off a lot of energy. When waves from the explosions hit Earth, they even affect compasses on planes and ships. These explosions, called flares, also shine brightly. So while the sunspots are somewhat cooler, around 8,000° F (4,500° C), flares are very hot. When the Sun is particularly "spotty," Earth is also a bit warmer than at other times.

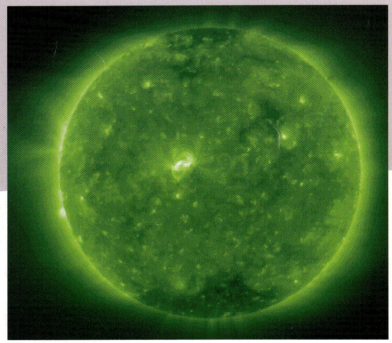

Above: A picture showing extremely hot gas in the Sun's corona, taken March 13, 1996, with the Extreme Ultraviolet Imaging Telescope aboard the *Solar and Heliospheric Observatory.*

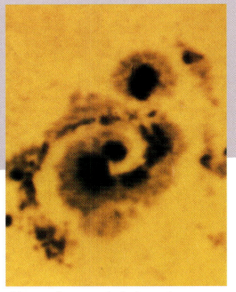

Above: A rare spiral-shaped sunspot. Normally, sunspots are seen as irregularly shaped dark holes. This unusual sunspot had a diameter 6 times that of Earth.

The hotter gases on the Sun's surface shine more brightly than the cooler gases. The cooler gases form dark areas called sunspots. The bright flashes pictured are called flares.

Left: A color-coded picture showing the structure of the Sun's hot, thin outer atmosphere, or corona. Just after the picture was taken, a flare erupted on the right edge of the Sun. Within minutes, the corona changed its shape.

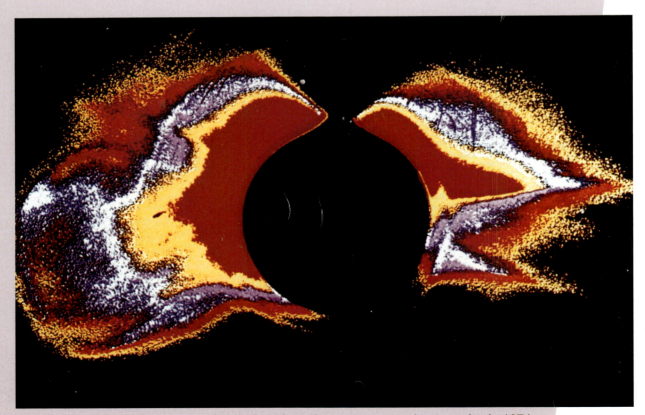

Above: This color-coded picture of emissions from the corona was taken one day in 1974. The emissions extended for millions of miles into space.

Graceful Prominences

Prominences are eruptions of gas held up by magnetic fields. Many people think they are among the most beautiful features of the Sun. Like sunspots, they are made of cooler gases. They lift off the Sun's surface into its hot thin outer atmosphere, which is called the corona. The gases of the prominence glow with red light and then sink down to the surface of the Sun. We can see these sheets of gas with special instruments. When viewed against the background of dark space, they may form graceful bright arches tens of thousands of miles high at the edge of the Sun. When seen against the background of the bright Sun, however, they may appear as relatively dark ribbons between sunspots. In this case, they are often called "filaments."

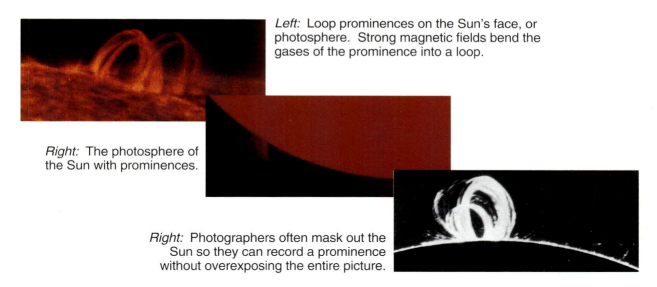

Left: Loop prominences on the Sun's face, or photosphere. Strong magnetic fields bend the gases of the prominence into a loop.

Right: The photosphere of the Sun with prominences.

Right: Photographers often mask out the Sun so they can record a prominence without overexposing the entire picture.

Does the Sun influence Earth?

Does the Sun influence Earth? Of course it does. Besides giving us light and warmth, there is the sunspot cycle. Every 11 years, the Sun gets very "spotty" at sunspot maximum and then almost clear of spots at sunspot minimum. That means the Sun gets a little warmer and then a little cooler. Does this strongly affect Earth's temperature, harvests, and rainfall? Possibly. Some people even think that the sunspot cycle might affect stock market prices, the ups and downs of the economy, and so on. It seems hard to believe, but is it possible?

A picture of the aurora borealis. Beneath the aurora is the Kitt Peak National Observatory in Arizona.

Above: A photo of the aurora borealis, or northern lights, over Alaska in the northern hemisphere. The aurora that is visible in the southern hemisphere is called aurora australis.

Colorful Lights of the Aurora

All this activity on the Sun's surface sends tiny particles outward in all directions. These particles, which carry electric charges, travel at speeds of hundreds of miles a second. This stream of particles is called the solar wind.

The solar wind reaches far out in space, passing by the various planets. When it reaches Earth, it collides with gas particles in the upper atmosphere, particularly near the North and South Poles.

Energy from this collision is released in the form of light. As a result, the polar nights are lit by faint-colored light in streamers and curves. This light is called the aurora. Sometimes, when the Sun is very active, the aurora can be seen beyond the polar regions.

In 2001, a space probe called *Genesis* was launched with the mission of obtaining samples of solar wind particles for study. The samples would be gathered in a region of space outside Earth's magnetosphere — the region influenced by Earth's magnetic field. Plans were for *Genesis* to return to Earth in 2004.

Above:
An artist's conception of the spacecraft *Genesis*, launched in 2001 to study solar wind.

Right: An artist's conception of solar wind seeping past and distorting a planet's magnetic field, from the *Solar and Heliospheric Observatory*.

An Eclipse of the Sun

Our Moon has helped us learn about the Sun. Sometimes the Sun seems to grow dark in the middle of a cloudless sky. This is because the Moon sometimes moves directly between us and the Sun. The Moon can sometimes block the entire body of the Sun, but the Sun's corona shines softly as a kind of halo around the Moon. This occurrence is called a total solar eclipse. It can last up to 7 1/2 minutes at the most before part of the Sun shows again. Since the Moon's shadow falls over just a small part of Earth in a total eclipse, any one area on Earth sees a total solar eclipse only about once every 300 years.

Total Solar Eclipse Timetable

Date	Location
December 4, 2002	Southern Africa, Southern Australia
November 23, 2003	Antarctica
April 8, 2005	Panama, Colombia
March 29, 2006	Central Africa, Turkey, Russia
August 1, 2008	Northern Canada, Siberia, China
July 22, 2009	India, Nepal, China
July 11, 2010	Chile, Argentina

The red giants — big, bigger, biggest

As large as the Sun is, it is not the largest star. Stars called red giants can be as much as 1,000 times as wide as the Sun, or more! Imagine that the Sun is in the center of a red giant, such as the one named Betelgeuse. That red giant would stretch past Mars. The matter that makes up red giant stars is spread very thinly. Even so, scientists think Betelgeuse may be as much as 18 to 20 times as massive as the Sun. Other stars are 90 to 100 times as massive as the Sun.

Above: During a total eclipse of the Sun, the Moon blocks the Sun's light from part of Earth. Within the area on Earth inside the smallest circle in this picture, the sky would be quite dark, and a person's view of the Sun would be that of the total solar eclipse. People within the outer circle would find daylight to be a strange kind of shadow, and for them the Sun would seem only partially eclipsed by the Moon.

This picture uses multiple images of the Sun to show the progress of a total solar eclipse that occurred in 1991.

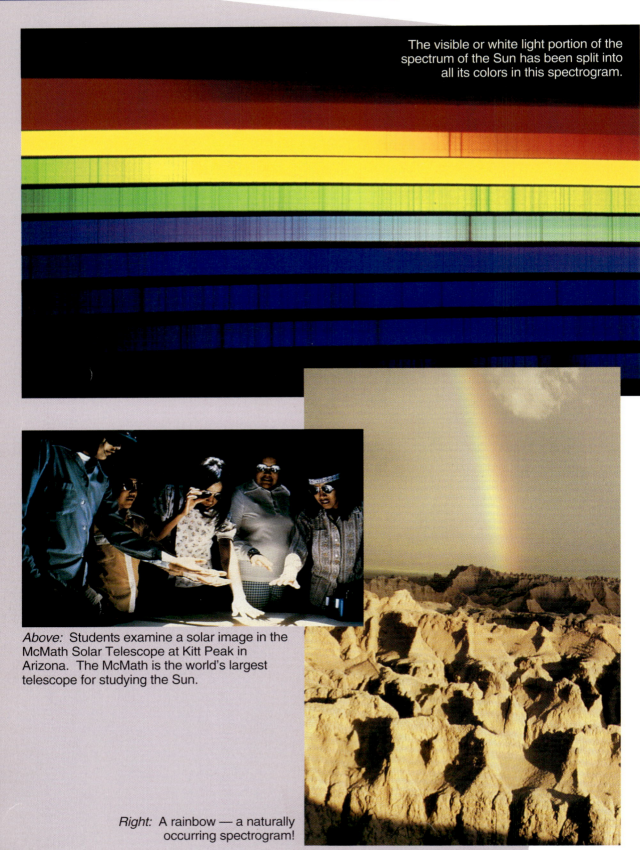

The visible or white light portion of the spectrum of the Sun has been split into all its colors in this spectrogram.

Above: Students examine a solar image in the McMath Solar Telescope at Kitt Peak in Arizona. The McMath is the world's largest telescope for studying the Sun.

Right: A rainbow — a naturally occurring spectrogram!

An Instrumental Way to Study the Sun

Most of the time, scientists use instruments to explore the Sun. Since the early 19th century, an instrument called the spectroscope has been used to study sunlight. It spreads light out into tiny wavelengths. The wavelengths have different colors. Beginning around 1890, scientists have also used an instrument called a spectroheliograph. This instrument reveals what elements are found in the Sun. A device called a coronagraph was introduced in 1931. It covers the bright light from the Sun's disk, so that scientists can examine the solar corona.

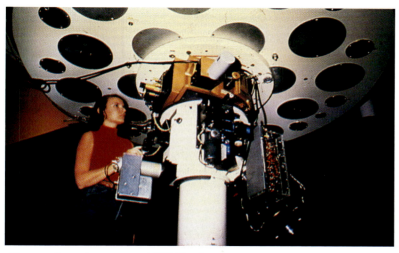

Above: An astronomer at Kitt Peak examines a spectroheliograph attached to a telescope.

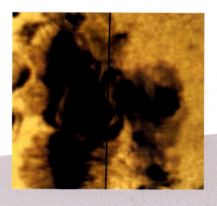

Sunspot pictures taken at Kitt Peak. Above: A white or natural light shot of the sunspot. *Left*: A spectrum shot of the sunspot.

Discovering the Sun's Secrets

Not all the radiation from the Sun reaches the surface of Earth. Our atmosphere absorbs much of it, so there is a lot about the Sun that we cannot know if we only look from Earth's surface. Various tools help us see the Sun from outside our atmosphere. Satellites carry instruments far above our atmosphere. For example, *Yohkoh*, a Japanese satellite launched into orbit around Earth in 1991, has made images of the Sun in the form of X rays. Its views of solar flares have provided important new information. The satellite *Ulysses*, launched in 1990, was placed in a special orbit that carries it far above the Sun's poles, which cannot be studied well from Earth. *Ulysses's* equipment included instruments for observing X rays and the solar wind. The European solar-orbiting satellite called *SOHO* (*Solar and Heliospheric Observatory*), which was launched in 1995, included instruments for studying the Sun in ultraviolet as well as visible light.

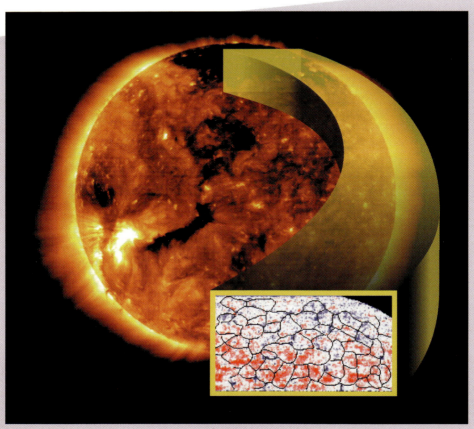

Left: This image from the *Solar and Heliospheric Observatory* shows where magnetic fields on the Sun are "open" and produce solar wind. The detailed close-up of one such "coronal hole" reveals a honeycomb pattern that delineates strong magnetic fields. Blue denotes gas moving outward and red inward.

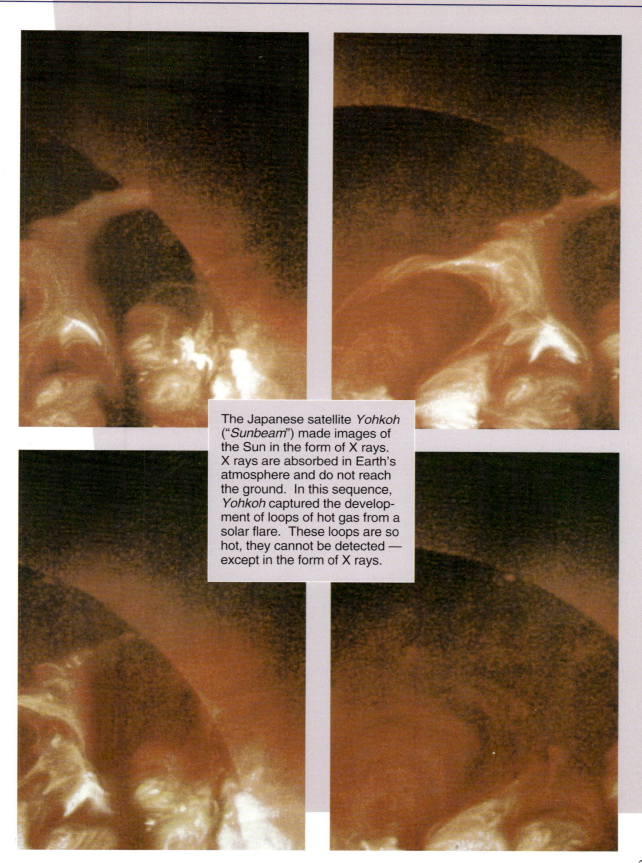

The Japanese satellite *Yohkoh* ("*Sunbeam*") made images of the Sun in the form of X rays. X rays are absorbed in Earth's atmosphere and do not reach the ground. In this sequence, *Yohkoh* captured the development of loops of hot gas from a solar flare. These loops are so hot, they cannot be detected — except in the form of X rays.

Above: The life and death of a star. This picture shows a star like our Sun passing through its life. From the nebula (*far left*) a cloud of gas and dust contracts into a solar nebula. The so-called protosun and surrounding disk (*rear, center*) take on the shape of our Sun and Solar System as we know them today (*rear, right*). Billions of years from now as the Sun loses energy, it will expand outward (*front, far right*), eventually becoming a red giant (*front*). Finally, its store of nuclear energy will be completely used up. It will collapse into a white dwarf (*front, left*) no bigger than Earth, and Earth itself will be little more than a dead, burned-up cinder.

Harnessing the Sun

There is still a great deal to find out about the Sun and how we can use it creatively on Earth. Scientists continue to study the sunspot cycle — the rise and fall in the number of sunspots from year to year. If they learn why the cycle takes place, they may learn more about what goes on deep inside the Sun. We have already learned how to harness some of the Sun's energy for heating Earth. Many buildings have special devices that capture the Sun's rays and store the heat for later use. These devices help conserve Earth's resources, such as coal and oil. Who knows what we might be able to do someday as we continue to unravel the mysteries of our star, the Sun?

Left: A small white star is in Earth's future. Imagine our Earth somewhere in time between the Sun as we know it now (*bottom*) and the tiny white dwarf it will someday become (*top*).

The case of the missing sunspots

It seems the sunspot cycle is not always with us. The Italian scientist Galileo discovered sunspots in 1610. Others observed them, too. Between 1645 and 1715, hardly a sunspot was seen on the Sun, however. After that, the familiar sunspot cycle began again. We call the spotless period between 1645 and 1715 a Maunder minimum, because an astronomer named Maunder discussed it in 1890. There may have been similar periods throughout history when sunspots were missing. What causes the cycle to suddenly stop and then restart? Astronomers are not sure.

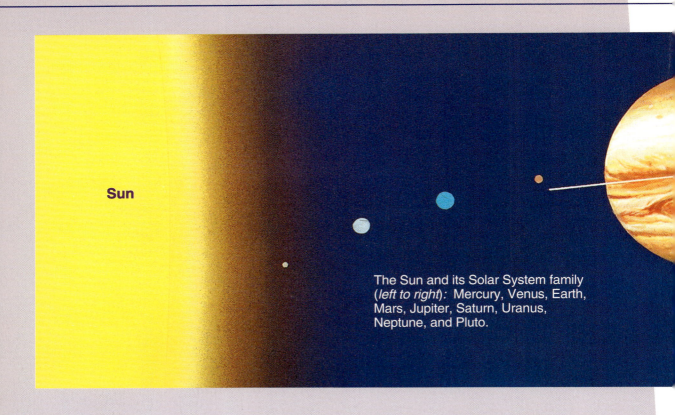

Sun

The Sun and its Solar System family (*left to right*): Mercury, Venus, Earth, Mars, Jupiter, Saturn, Uranus, Neptune, and Pluto.

Fact File: Our Sustaining Sun

The Sun is, of course, our very own star. As far as stars go, though, the Sun is not all that big. Its diameter is about 109 times that of Earth. It is about 270,000 times closer to Earth than is Proxima Centauri, the next closest star. So our Sun looks quite big to us here on Earth. While the light from Proxima Centauri takes over 4 years to reach Earth, the light from the Sun takes only about 8 minutes. So, although the Sun is small compared to many stars, its size and distance from Earth have combined to sustain life on our planet.

Right: A close-up of the Sun and
some of its special features.

The Sun versus Earth

Object	Diameter	Rotation Period (length of day)	Period of Orbit around Sun (length of year)	Surface Gravity	Distance from Sun (nearest–farthest)	Least Time for Light to Reach Earth
Sun	865,000 miles (1,392,000 km)	25–36 days*	—	28**	—	8.2 minutes
Earth	7,927 miles (12,756 km)	23 hours, 56 minutes	365.256 days (1 year)	1**	91.3–94.4 million miles (147–152 million km)	—

* At its surface, the Sun rotates faster near the poles than at the equator; deep inside, the rotation period is 27 days.
** Multiply your weight by this number to find out how much you would weigh on these celestial objects.

29

More Books about the Sun

DK Space Encyclopedia. Nigel Henbest and Heather Couper (DK Publishing)

A Look at the Sun. Ray Spangenburg and Kit Moser (Franklin Watts)

Secrets of the Sun: A Closer Look at Our Star. Patricia L. Barnes-Svarney (Raintree/Steck Vaughn)

The Sun. Gregory Vogt (Bridgestone Books)

The Sun: The Center of the Solar System. Michael D. Cole (Enslow)

When the Sun Dies. Ray A. Gallant (Marshall Cavendish)

CD-ROMs

Exploring the Planets. (Cinegram)

Web Sites

The Internet is a good place to get more information about the Sun. The web sites listed here can help you learn about the most recent discoveries, as well as those made in the past.

Genesis Search for Origins. www.genesismission.org

Nine Planets. www.nineplanets.org/sol.html

SOHO Exploring the Sun. sohowww.nascom.nasa.gov/

Stanford Solar Center. solar-center.stanford.edu

Views of the Solar System. www.solarviews.com/eng/sun.htm

Windows to the Universe. www.windows.ucar.edu/tour/link=/sun/sun.html

Places to Visit

Here are some museums and centers where you can find a variety of space exhibits.

American Museum of Natural History
Central Park West at 79th Street
New York, NY 10024

Canada Science and Technology Museum
1867 St. Laurent Boulevard
Science Park
100 Queen's Park
Ottawa, Ontario K1G 5A3
Canada

Henry Crown Space Center
Museum of Science and Industry
57th Street and Lake Shore Drive
Chicago, IL 60637

National Air and Space Museum
Smithsonian Institution
7th and Independence Avenue SW
Washington, DC 20560

Odyssium
11211 142nd Street
Edmonton, Alberta T5M 4A1
Canada

Scienceworks Museum
2 Booker Street
Spotswood
Melbourne, Victoria 3015
Australia

Glossary

asteroids: very small "planets." Hundreds of thousands of them exist in our Solar System. Most of them orbit the Sun between Mars and Jupiter, but many occur elsewhere.

aurora: light near the North and South Poles and sometimes elsewhere caused by the collision of the solar wind with Earth's upper atmosphere.

axis: the imaginary straight line around which a planet, star, or moon turns or rotates.

corona: the hot thin outer atmosphere of the Sun.

ESA: the European Space Agency.

flares: explosions near sunspots that give off great energy.

fusion: the coming together of hydrogen atoms to form helium. Fusion produces enormous energy.

granule: one of the cell-like spots on the Sun's surface that disappear after a brief time, usually about eight minutes. An average granule is about 600 miles (1,000 km) in diameter.

gravity: the force that causes objects like the Sun and its planets to be attracted to one another.

helium: a gas formed in the Sun by the fusion of hydrogen atoms.

hydrogen: a colorless, odorless gas that is the simplest and lightest of the elements. The Sun is about three-quarters hydrogen.

NASA: the National Aeronautics and Space Administration. The government space agency in the United States.

neutrinos: very tiny particles produced when hydrogen fuses to helium in the center of the Sun. They fly out in all directions.

orbit: the path that one celestial object follows as it circles, or revolves around, another.

planet: one of the large bodies that revolve around a star like our Sun. Our Earth is one of the planets in our Solar System.

pole: either end of the axis around which a planet, moon, or star rotates.

prominences: eruptions of relatively cool gas into the corona. When seen against the bright disk of the Sun, they may look like dark ribbons, or "filaments," between sunspots. When viewed against the dark sky, they look brighter, sometimes taking the form of loops.

radio telescope: an instrument that uses a radio receiver and antenna to both see into space and listen for messages from space.

red giants: huge stars whose diameter may be as much as a thousand times greater than that of the Sun.

rotate: to turn, or spin, on an axis.

Solar System: the Sun with the planets and all the other bodies, such as the asteroids, that orbit the Sun.

solar wind: tiny particles that travel from the Sun's surface at speeds of hundreds of miles a second.

spectroscope, spectrohelio-graph, and coronagraph: devices used by scientists to study the Sun.

Sun: our star and the provider of the energy that makes life possible on Earth.

sunspot: a dark area on the Sun caused by gases that are cooler and shine less brightly than the hotter surrounding gases.

total solar eclipse: the blocking of the entire body of the Sun by the Moon.

Index

Born in 1920, Isaac Asimov came to the United States as a young boy from his native Russia. As a young man, he was a student of biochemistry. In time, he became one of the most productive writers the world has ever known. His books cover a spectrum of topics, including science, history, language theory, fantasy, and science fiction. His brilliant imagination gained him the respect and admiration of adults and children alike. Sadly, Isaac Asimov died shortly after the publication of the first edition of *Isaac Asimov's Library of the Universe.*

The publishers wish to thank the following for permission to reproduce copyright material: front cover, 3, 6 (lower left), 8, 9 (upper), 14 (left), 19 (lower), 24, ESA/NASA; 4 (all), © Julian Baum 1987; 5, © Anglo-Australian Observatory Telescope Board 1981; 6 (upper), Defense Nuclear Agency; 6 (lower right), Brookhaven National Laboratory; 7, © Lynette Cook 1987; 9 (lower), © Julian Baum 1987; 10, 11, British Museum, Michael Holford Photographs; 12, 13, Big Bear Solar Observatory; 14 (right), National Optical Astronomy Observatories; 15, © Sally Bensusen 1987; 16 (both), NASA; 17 (upper), NASA; 17 (center), © George East; 17 (lower), Defense Nuclear Agency; 18 (large), Adam Block/NOAO/AURA/NSF; 18 (inset), © Forrest Baldwin; 19 (upper), NASA; 21 (upper), © Sally Bensusen 1987; 21 (lower), © William Sterne; 22 (upper and lower left), National Optical Astronomy Observatories; 22 (lower right), © James Peterson; 23 (all), National Optical Astronomy Observatories; 25 (all), S. Taylor, Lockheed, Palo Alto Research Laboratories; 26, © Brian Sullivan 1988; 27, © Doug McLeod; 28-29, 29, © Sally Bensusen 1987.